THIS JOURNAL BELONGS TO:

Campground:

Dates: FROM _____ TO _____

Location: _____

We stayed at site number: _____

Weather:

Score: 1 2 3 4 5 6 7 8 9 10

Who was on this trip with us: _____

Our favorite activity was: _____

The most memorable thing about this trip was: _____

The most fun thing about this trip was: _____

Next time we come back, we must remember to: _____

Our favorite things and places to eat: _____

Other Notes:

_____
_____
_____
_____
_____
_____
_____
_____
_____
_____

A drawing or photo of the favorite part of our stay:

Campground:_____

FROM   TO
Dates:_____   _____

Location: _____

_____ We stayed at site number: _____

Weather: Score:
1 2 3 4 5 6 7 8 9 10

Who was on this trip with us: _____

_____

_____

Our favorite activity was: _____

_____

_____

The most memorable thing about this trip was: _____

_____

_____

The most fun thing about this trip was: _____

_____

_____

Next time we come back, we must remember to: _____

_____

_____

Our favorite things and places to eat: _____

_____

_____

Other Notes:

A drawing or photo of the favorite part of our stay:

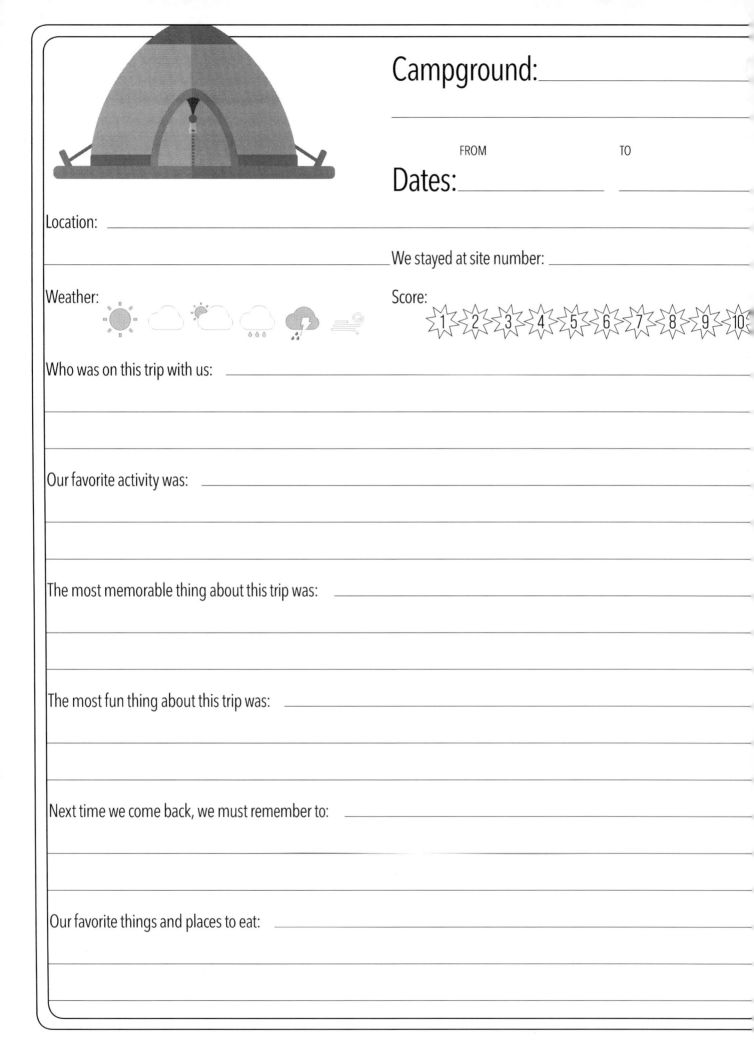

Campground: _____

_____

FROM _____ TO _____

Dates: _____ _____

Location: _____

_____

We stayed at site number: _____

Weather:

Score: 1 2 3 4 5 6 7 8 9 10

Who was on this trip with us: _____

_____

_____

Our favorite activity was: _____

_____

_____

The most memorable thing about this trip was: _____

_____

_____

The most fun thing about this trip was: _____

_____

_____

Next time we come back, we must remember to: _____

_____

_____

Our favorite things and places to eat: _____

_____

Other Notes:

A drawing or photo of the favorite part of our stay:

Campground:_____

_____

FROM   TO

Dates:_____   _____

Location: _____

_____ We stayed at site number: _____

Weather: Score: 1 2 3 4 5 6 7 8 9 10

Who was on this trip with us: _____

_____

_____

Our favorite activity was: _____

_____

_____

The most memorable thing about this trip was: _____

_____

_____

The most fun thing about this trip was: _____

_____

_____

Next time we come back, we must remember to: _____

_____

_____

Our favorite things and places to eat: _____

_____

_____

Other Notes:

_____
_____
_____
_____
_____
_____
_____
_____
_____
_____

A drawing or photo of the favorite part of our stay:

Campground:_____

_____

FROM   TO

Dates:_____   _____

Location: _____

_____

We stayed at site number: _____

Weather:

Score:

1 2 3 4 5 6 7 8 9 10

Who was on this trip with us: _____

_____

_____

Our favorite activity was: _____

_____

_____

The most memorable thing about this trip was: _____

_____

_____

The most fun thing about this trip was: _____

_____

_____

Next time we come back, we must remember to: _____

_____

_____

Our favorite things and places to eat: _____

_____

_____

Other Notes:

_____
_____
_____
_____
_____
_____
_____
_____

A drawing or photo of the favorite part of our stay:

Campground:_____

_____

FROM   TO

Dates:_____   _____

Location: _____

_____

We stayed at site number: _____

Weather: ☀ ☁ ⛅ 🌧 ⛈ 🌬

Score: 1 2 3 4 5 6 7 8 9 10

Who was on this trip with us: _____

_____

_____

Our favorite activity was: _____

_____

_____

The most memorable thing about this trip was: _____

_____

_____

The most fun thing about this trip was: _____

_____

_____

Next time we come back, we must remember to: _____

_____

_____

Our favorite things and places to eat: _____

_____

_____

Other Notes:

A drawing or photo of the favorite part of our stay:

Campground:_____

FROM   TO

Dates:_____   _____

Location: _____

_____ We stayed at site number: _____

Weather: Score:

1 2 3 4 5 6 7 8 9 10

Who was on this trip with us: _____

_____

_____

Our favorite activity was: _____

_____

_____

The most memorable thing about this trip was: _____

_____

_____

_____

The most fun thing about this trip was: _____

_____

_____

_____

Next time we come back, we must remember to: _____

_____

_____

_____

Our favorite things and places to eat: _____

_____

_____

Other Notes:

_____
_____
_____
_____
_____
_____
_____
_____
_____
_____

A drawing or photo of the favorite part of our stay:

Campground:_____

_____

FROM   TO

Dates:_____   _____

Location: _____

_____ We stayed at site number: _____

Weather: Score:

1 2 3 4 5 6 7 8 9 10

Who was on this trip with us: _____

_____

_____

Our favorite activity was: _____

_____

_____

The most memorable thing about this trip was: _____

_____

_____

The most fun thing about this trip was: _____

_____

_____

Next time we come back, we must remember to: _____

_____

_____

Our favorite things and places to eat: _____

_____

_____

Other Notes:

A drawing or photo of the favorite part of our stay:

Campground:_____

Dates:_____ _____
          FROM   TO

Location: _____

We stayed at site number: _____

Weather: ☀ ☁ ⛅ 🌧 ⛈ 🌬

Score: 1 2 3 4 5 6 7 8 9 10

Who was on this trip with us: _____

Our favorite activity was: _____

The most memorable thing about this trip was: _____

The most fun thing about this trip was: _____

Next time we come back, we must remember to: _____

Our favorite things and places to eat: _____

Other Notes:

A drawing or photo of the favorite part of our stay:

Campground:_____

_____

FROM   TO

Dates:_____ _____

Location: _____

We stayed at site number: _____

Weather: ☀ ☁ ⛅ 🌧 ⛈ 🌬

Score: 1 2 3 4 5 6 7 8 9 10

Who was on this trip with us: _____

_____

_____

Our favorite activity was: _____

_____

_____

The most memorable thing about this trip was: _____

_____

_____

The most fun thing about this trip was: _____

_____

_____

Next time we come back, we must remember to: _____

_____

_____

Our favorite things and places to eat: _____

_____

_____

Other Notes:

A drawing or photo of the favorite part of our stay:

Campground:

Dates: FROM _____ TO _____

Location: _____

_____

We stayed at site number: _____

Weather:

Score: 1 2 3 4 5 6 7 8 9 10

Who was on this trip with us: _____

_____

_____

Our favorite activity was: _____

_____

_____

The most memorable thing about this trip was: _____

_____

_____

The most fun thing about this trip was: _____

_____

_____

Next time we come back, we must remember to: _____

_____

_____

Our favorite things and places to eat: _____

_____

_____

Other Notes:

A drawing or photo of the favorite part of our stay:

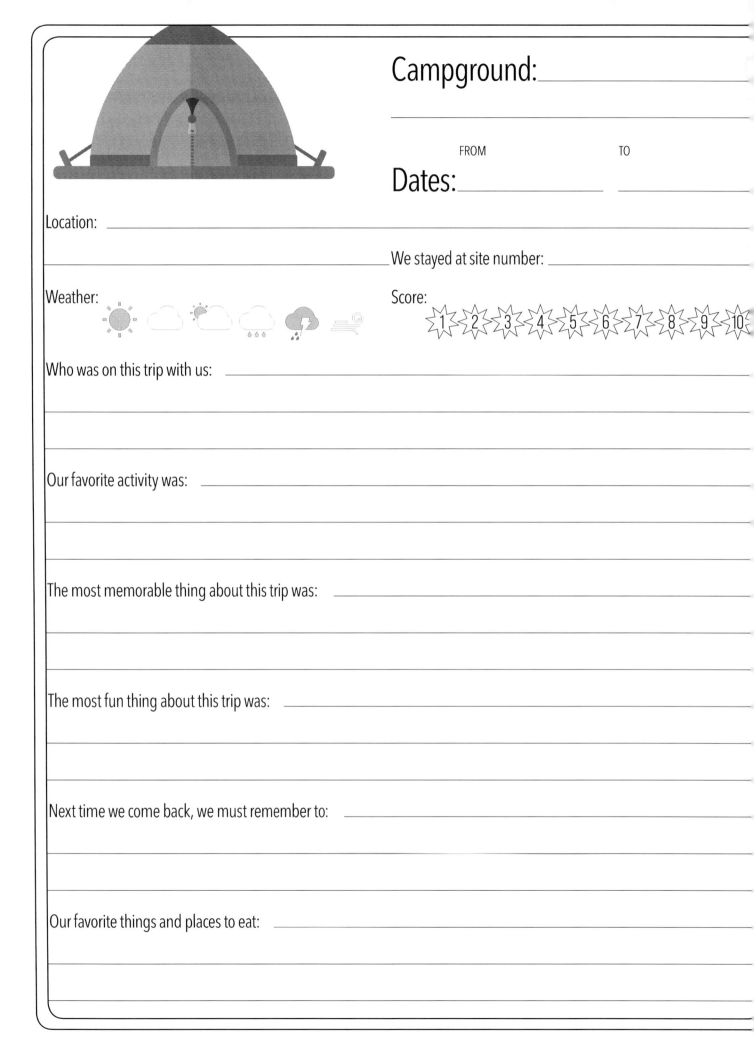

Campground:

FROM   TO

Dates:

Location: _____

_____ We stayed at site number: _____

Weather: Score:

1 2 3 4 5 6 7 8 9 10

Who was on this trip with us: _____

_____

_____

Our favorite activity was: _____

_____

_____

The most memorable thing about this trip was: _____

_____

_____

The most fun thing about this trip was: _____

_____

_____

Next time we come back, we must remember to: _____

_____

_____

Our favorite things and places to eat: _____

_____

_____

Other Notes:

A drawing or photo of the favorite part of our stay:

Campground:_____

_____

FROM   TO

Dates:_____   _____

Location:_____

_____

We stayed at site number:_____

Weather:

Score: 1 2 3 4 5 6 7 8 9 10

Who was on this trip with us:_____

_____

_____

Our favorite activity was:_____

_____

_____

The most memorable thing about this trip was:_____

_____

_____

The most fun thing about this trip was:_____

_____

_____

Next time we come back, we must remember to:_____

_____

_____

Our favorite things and places to eat:_____

_____

Other Notes:

_____

_____

_____

_____

_____

_____

_____

_____

_____

A drawing or photo of the favorite part of our stay:

Campground:_____

_____

FROM   TO

Dates:_____   _____

Location: _____

_____ We stayed at site number: _____

Weather: ☀ ☁ ⛅ 🌧 ⛈ 🌬

Score: 1 2 3 4 5 6 7 8 9 10

Who was on this trip with us: _____

_____

_____

Our favorite activity was: _____

_____

_____

The most memorable thing about this trip was: _____

_____

_____

The most fun thing about this trip was: _____

_____

_____

Next time we come back, we must remember to: _____

_____

_____

Our favorite things and places to eat: _____

_____

_____

Other Notes:

_____
_____
_____
_____
_____
_____
_____
_____
_____

A drawing or photo of the favorite part of our stay:

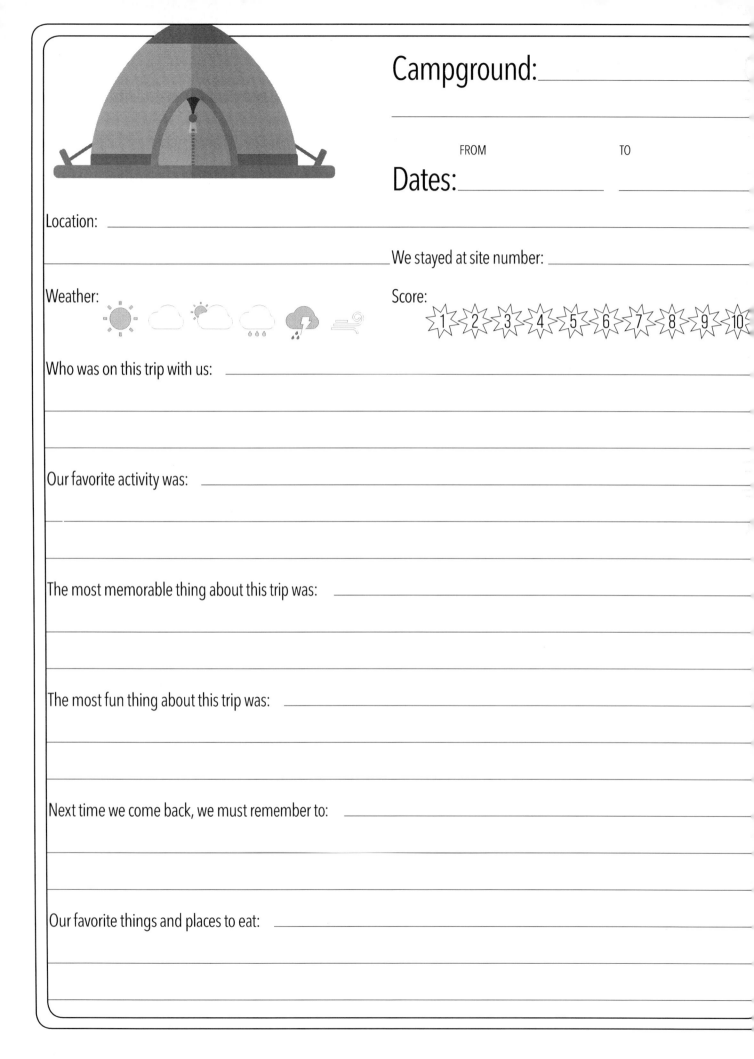

Campground:_____

_____

FROM   TO

Dates:_____   _____

Location: _____

_____ We stayed at site number: _____

Weather: Score:

1 2 3 4 5 6 7 8 9 10

Who was on this trip with us: _____

_____

_____

Our favorite activity was: _____

_____

_____

The most memorable thing about this trip was: _____

_____

_____

The most fun thing about this trip was: _____

_____

_____

Next time we come back, we must remember to: _____

_____

_____

Our favorite things and places to eat: _____

_____

_____

Other Notes:

_____

_____

_____

_____

_____

_____

_____

_____

A drawing or photo of the favorite part of our stay:

Campground:

FROM   TO

Dates:

Location:

We stayed at site number:

Weather:

Score: 1 2 3 4 5 6 7 8 9 10

Who was on this trip with us:

Our favorite activity was:

The most memorable thing about this trip was:

The most fun thing about this trip was:

Next time we come back, we must remember to:

Our favorite things and places to eat:

Other Notes:

_____
_____
_____
_____
_____
_____
_____
_____

A drawing or photo of the favorite part of our stay:

Campground:_____

_____

FROM   TO

Dates:_____   _____

Location: _____

_____ We stayed at site number: _____

Weather: Score:

1   2   3   4   5   6   7   8   9   10

Who was on this trip with us: _____

_____

_____

Our favorite activity was: _____

_____

_____

The most memorable thing about this trip was: _____

_____

_____

The most fun thing about this trip was: _____

_____

_____

Next time we come back, we must remember to: _____

_____

_____

Our favorite things and places to eat: _____

_____

_____

Other Notes:

_____
_____
_____
_____
_____
_____
_____
_____
_____

A drawing or photo of the favorite part of our stay:

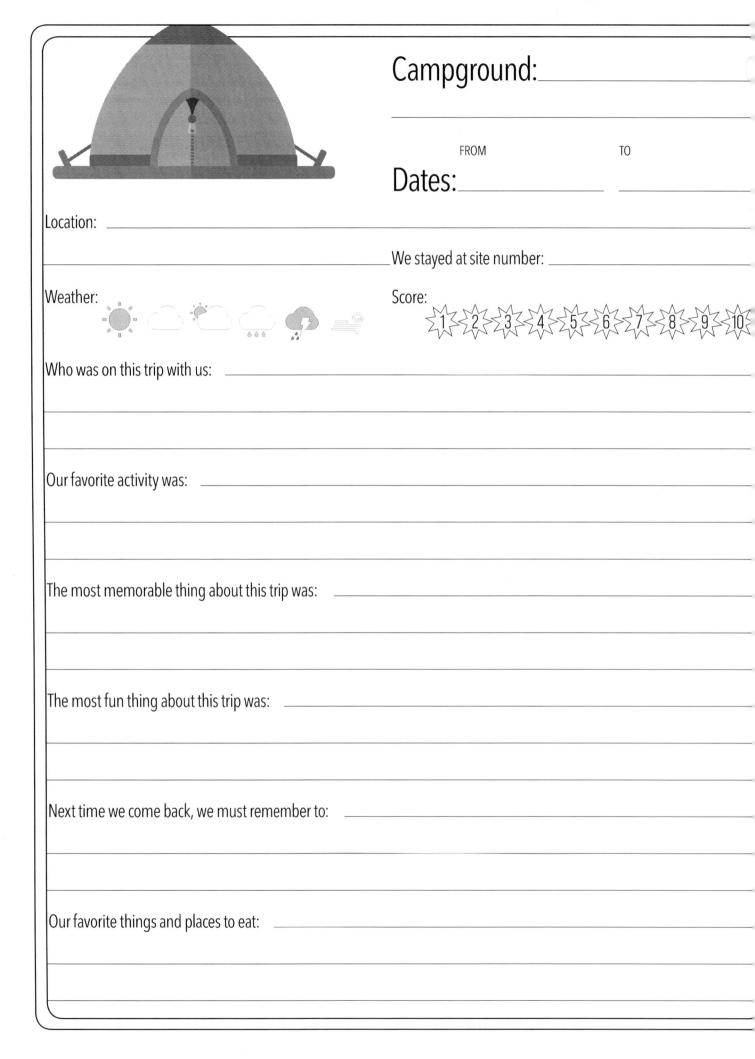

Campground:_____

_____

FROM   TO

Dates:_____   _____

Location: _____

_____ We stayed at site number: _____

Weather: Score:

1 2 3 4 5 6 7 8 9 10

Who was on this trip with us: _____

_____

_____

Our favorite activity was: _____

_____

_____

The most memorable thing about this trip was: _____

_____

_____

The most fun thing about this trip was: _____

_____

_____

Next time we come back, we must remember to: _____

_____

_____

Our favorite things and places to eat: _____

_____

_____

Other Notes:

_____
_____
_____
_____
_____
_____
_____
_____
_____

A drawing or photo of the favorite part of our stay:

Campground:

FROM TO

Dates:

Location:

We stayed at site number:

Weather:

Score: 1 2 3 4 5 6 7 8 9 10

Who was on this trip with us:

Our favorite activity was:

The most memorable thing about this trip was:

The most fun thing about this trip was:

Next time we come back, we must remember to:

Our favorite things and places to eat:

Other Notes:

A drawing or photo of the favorite part of our stay:

Campground:_____

_____

FROM   TO

Dates:_____   _____

Location: _____

_____ We stayed at site number: _____

Weather: ☀ ☁ ⛅ 🌧 ⛈ 🌬   Score: 1 2 3 4 5 6 7 8 9 10

Who was on this trip with us: _____

_____

_____

Our favorite activity was: _____

_____

_____

The most memorable thing about this trip was: _____

_____

_____

The most fun thing about this trip was: _____

_____

_____

Next time we come back, we must remember to: _____

_____

_____

Our favorite things and places to eat: _____

_____

Other Notes:

A drawing or photo of the favorite part of our stay:

Campground:_____

_____

FROM   TO

Dates:_____   _____

Location: _____

_____ We stayed at site number: _____

Weather: Score:

1 2 3 4 5 6 7 8 9 10

Who was on this trip with us: _____

_____

_____

Our favorite activity was: _____

_____

_____

The most memorable thing about this trip was: _____

_____

_____

The most fun thing about this trip was: _____

_____

_____

Next time we come back, we must remember to: _____

_____

_____

Our favorite things and places to eat: _____

_____

_____

Other Notes:

A drawing or photo of the favorite part of our stay:

Campground:_____

_____

FROM   TO

Dates:_____   _____

Location: _____

_____ We stayed at site number: _____

Weather: Score:

1 2 3 4 5 6 7 8 9 10

Who was on this trip with us: _____

_____

_____

Our favorite activity was: _____

_____

_____

The most memorable thing about this trip was: _____

_____

_____

The most fun thing about this trip was: _____

_____

_____

Next time we come back, we must remember to: _____

_____

_____

Our favorite things and places to eat: _____

_____

_____

Other Notes:

_____

_____

_____

_____

_____

_____

_____

_____

_____

_____

A drawing or photo of the favorite part of our stay:

Campground:_____

_____

FROM   TO

Dates:_____   _____

Location: _____

_____ We stayed at site number: _____

Weather: Score:

1 2 3 4 5 6 7 8 9 10

Who was on this trip with us: _____

_____

_____

Our favorite activity was: _____

_____

_____

The most memorable thing about this trip was: _____

_____

_____

The most fun thing about this trip was: _____

_____

_____

Next time we come back, we must remember to: _____

_____

_____

Our favorite things and places to eat: _____

_____

Other Notes:

A drawing or photo of the favorite part of our stay:

Campground:

FROM   TO

Dates:

Location:

We stayed at site number:

Weather: Score:

1 2 3 4 5 6 7 8 9 10

Who was on this trip with us:

Our favorite activity was:

The most memorable thing about this trip was:

The most fun thing about this trip was:

Next time we come back, we must remember to:

Our favorite things and places to eat:

Other Notes:

A drawing or photo of the favorite part of our stay:

Campground:

FROM   TO

Dates:

Location:

We stayed at site number:

Weather:

Score:
1 2 3 4 5 6 7 8 9 10

Who was on this trip with us:

Our favorite activity was:

The most memorable thing about this trip was:

The most fun thing about this trip was:

Next time we come back, we must remember to:

Our favorite things and places to eat:

Other Notes:

A drawing or photo of the favorite part of our stay:

Campground:_____

FROM   TO

Dates:_____ _____

Location: _____

We stayed at site number: _____

Weather: ☀ ☁ ⛅ 🌧 ⛈ 🌬

Score: 1 2 3 4 5 6 7 8 9 10

Who was on this trip with us: _____

_____

_____

Our favorite activity was: _____

_____

_____

The most memorable thing about this trip was: _____

_____

_____

The most fun thing about this trip was: _____

_____

_____

Next time we come back, we must remember to: _____

_____

_____

Our favorite things and places to eat: _____

_____

_____

Other Notes:

A drawing or photo of the favorite part of our stay:

Campground:_____

_____

FROM   TO

Dates:_____   _____

Location: _____

_____

We stayed at site number: _____

Weather:

Score:

1 2 3 4 5 6 7 8 9 10

Who was on this trip with us: _____

_____

_____

Our favorite activity was: _____

_____

_____

The most memorable thing about this trip was: _____

_____

_____

The most fun thing about this trip was: _____

_____

_____

Next time we come back, we must remember to: _____

_____

_____

Our favorite things and places to eat: _____

_____

Other Notes:

_____
_____
_____
_____
_____
_____
_____
_____
_____

A drawing or photo of the favorite part of our stay:

Campground:_____

_____

FROM   TO

Dates:_____   _____

Location: _____

_____ We stayed at site number: _____

Weather: Score:

1 2 3 4 5 6 7 8 9 10

Who was on this trip with us: _____

_____

_____

Our favorite activity was: _____

_____

_____

The most memorable thing about this trip was: _____

_____

_____

The most fun thing about this trip was: _____

_____

_____

Next time we come back, we must remember to: _____

_____

_____

Our favorite things and places to eat: _____

_____

Other Notes:

A drawing or photo of the favorite part of our stay:

Campground:_____

_____

FROM   TO

Dates:_____ _____

Location: _____

_____ We stayed at site number: _____

Weather:

Score:

1 2 3 4 5 6 7 8 9 10

Who was on this trip with us: _____

_____

_____

Our favorite activity was: _____

_____

_____

The most memorable thing about this trip was: _____

_____

_____

The most fun thing about this trip was: _____

_____

_____

Next time we come back, we must remember to: _____

_____

_____

Our favorite things and places to eat: _____

_____

_____

Other Notes:

A drawing or photo of the favorite part of our stay:

Campground:

Dates: FROM _____ TO _____

Location: _____

We stayed at site number: _____

Weather: ☀ ☁ ⛅ 🌧 ⛈ 🌬

Score: 1 2 3 4 5 6 7 8 9 10

Who was on this trip with us: _____

Our favorite activity was: _____

The most memorable thing about this trip was: _____

The most fun thing about this trip was: _____

Next time we come back, we must remember to: _____

Our favorite things and places to eat: _____

Other Notes:

A drawing or photo of the favorite part of our stay:

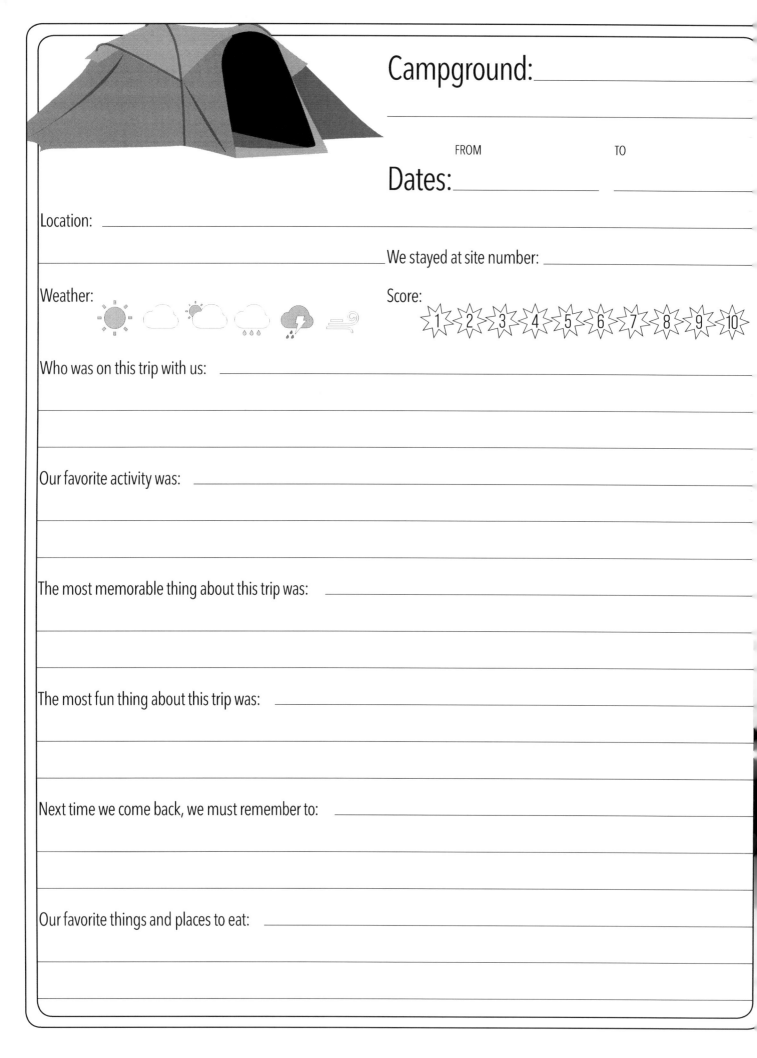

Campground:

FROM   TO

Dates:

Location:

We stayed at site number:

Weather:

Score: 1 2 3 4 5 6 7 8 9 10

Who was on this trip with us:

Our favorite activity was:

The most memorable thing about this trip was:

The most fun thing about this trip was:

Next time we come back, we must remember to:

Our favorite things and places to eat:

Other Notes:

_____
_____
_____
_____
_____
_____
_____
_____
_____

A drawing or photo of the favorite part of our stay:

Campground:_____

FROM   TO
Dates:_____ _____

Location: _____

_____ We stayed at site number: _____

Weather: Score:
                                  1 2 3 4 5 6 7 8 9 10

Who was on this trip with us: _____

_____

_____

Our favorite activity was: _____

_____

_____

The most memorable thing about this trip was: _____

_____

_____

The most fun thing about this trip was: _____

_____

_____

Next time we come back, we must remember to: _____

_____

_____

Our favorite things and places to eat: _____

_____

_____

Other Notes:

_____

_____

_____

_____

_____

_____

_____

_____

_____

A drawing or photo of the favorite part of our stay:

Campground:

Dates:
FROM _____ TO _____

Location: _____

We stayed at site number: _____

Weather:

Score: 1 2 3 4 5 6 7 8 9 10

Who was on this trip with us: _____

Our favorite activity was: _____

The most memorable thing about this trip was: _____

The most fun thing about this trip was: _____

Next time we come back, we must remember to: _____

Our favorite things and places to eat: _____

Other Notes:

A drawing or photo of the favorite part of our stay:

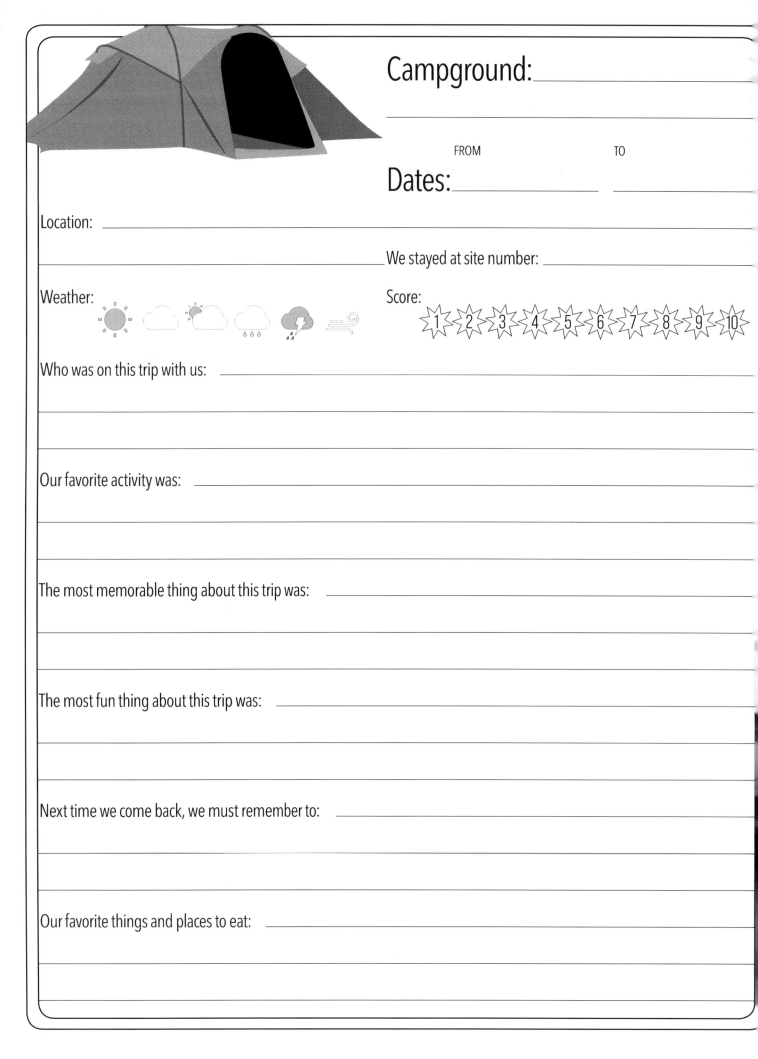

Campground: _____

_____

FROM _____ TO _____

Dates: _____

Location: _____

_____ We stayed at site number: _____

Weather: ☀ ☁ ⛅ 🌧 ⛈ 🌬

Score: 1 2 3 4 5 6 7 8 9 10

Who was on this trip with us: _____

Our favorite activity was: _____

The most memorable thing about this trip was: _____

The most fun thing about this trip was: _____

Next time we come back, we must remember to: _____

Our favorite things and places to eat: _____

Other Notes:

A drawing or photo of the favorite part of our stay:

Campground: _____

FROM _____ TO _____

Dates: _____ _____

Location: _____

We stayed at site number: _____

Weather:

Score: 1 2 3 4 5 6 7 8 9 10

Who was on this trip with us: _____

Our favorite activity was: _____

The most memorable thing about this trip was: _____

The most fun thing about this trip was: _____

Next time we come back, we must remember to: _____

Our favorite things and places to eat: _____

Other Notes:

_____

_____

_____

_____

_____

_____

_____

_____

_____

A drawing or photo of the favorite part of our stay:

Campground:

FROM   TO

Dates:

Location:

We stayed at site number:

Weather:

Score: 1 2 3 4 5 6 7 8 9 10

Who was on this trip with us:

Our favorite activity was:

The most memorable thing about this trip was:

The most fun thing about this trip was:

Next time we come back, we must remember to:

Our favorite things and places to eat:

Other Notes:

A drawing or photo of the favorite part of our stay:

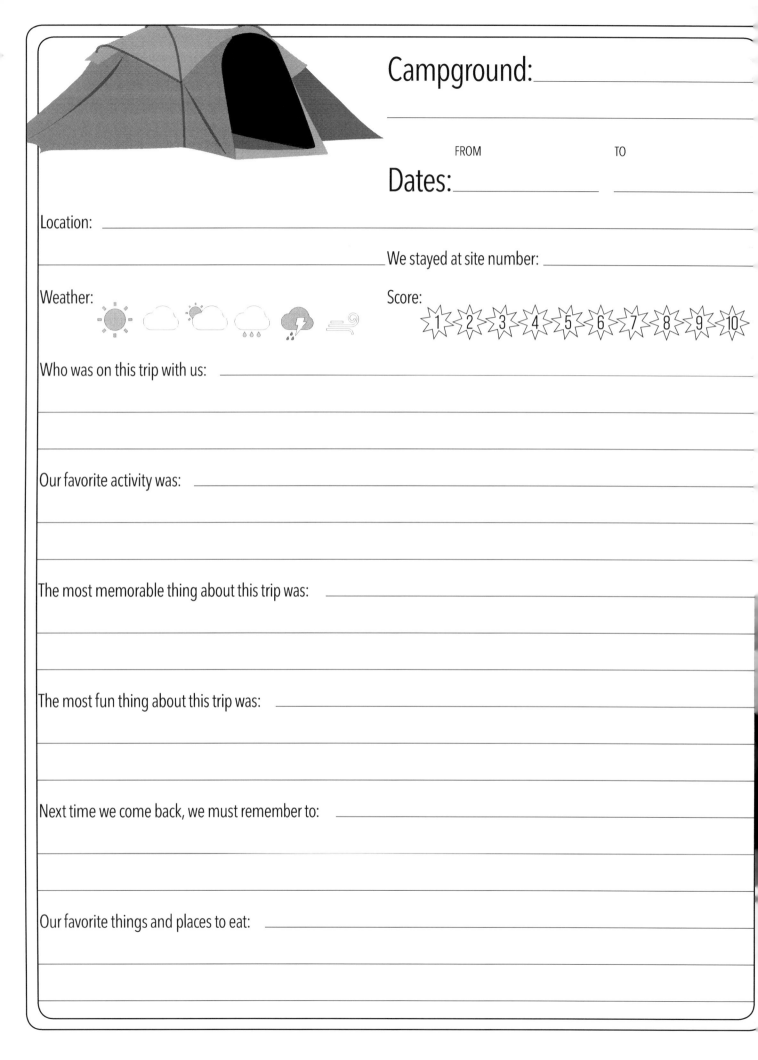

Campground:_____

_____

FROM   TO
Dates:_____   _____

Location: _____

_____

We stayed at site number: _____

Weather: Score: 1 2 3 4 5 6 7 8 9 10

Who was on this trip with us: _____

_____

_____

Our favorite activity was: _____

_____

_____

The most memorable thing about this trip was: _____

_____

_____

The most fun thing about this trip was: _____

_____

_____

Next time we come back, we must remember to: _____

_____

_____

Our favorite things and places to eat: _____

_____

_____

Other Notes:

A drawing or photo of the favorite part of our stay:

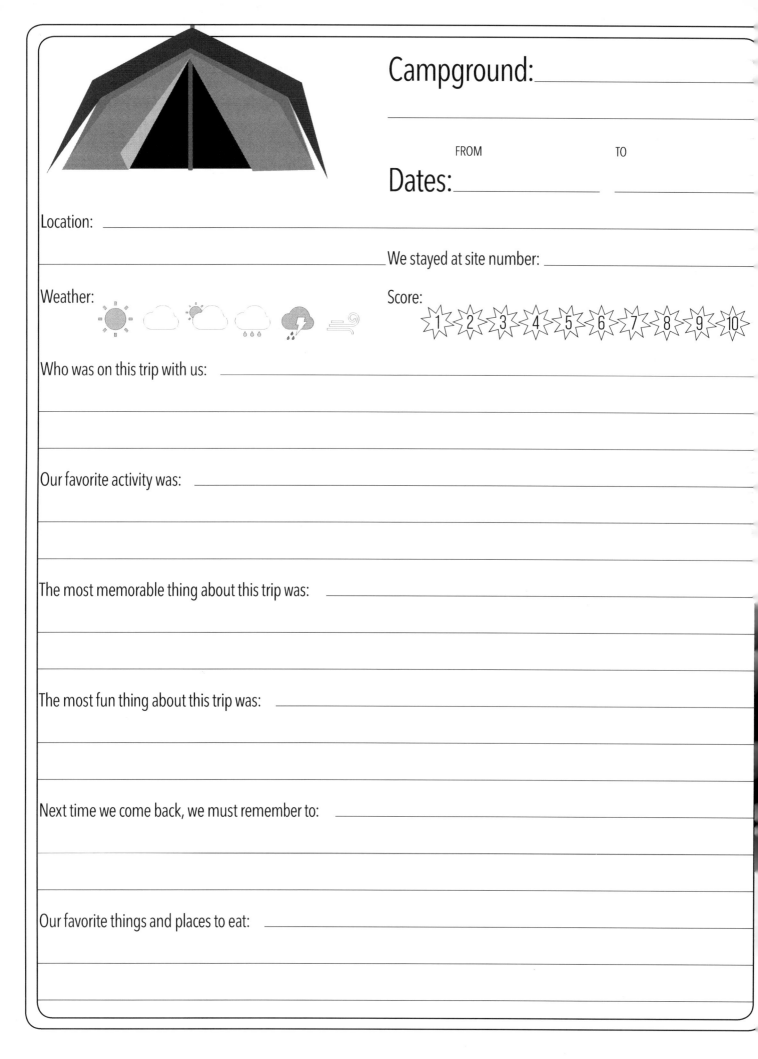

Campground: _____

FROM   TO

Dates: _____   _____

Location: _____

We stayed at site number: _____

Weather:

Score: 1 2 3 4 5 6 7 8 9 10

Who was on this trip with us: _____

Our favorite activity was: _____

The most memorable thing about this trip was: _____

The most fun thing about this trip was: _____

Next time we come back, we must remember to: _____

Our favorite things and places to eat: _____

Other Notes:

A drawing or photo of the favorite part of our stay:

Campground:

FROM   TO

Dates:

Location:

We stayed at site number:

Weather:

Score: 1 2 3 4 5 6 7 8 9 10

Who was on this trip with us:

Our favorite activity was:

The most memorable thing about this trip was:

The most fun thing about this trip was:

Next time we come back, we must remember to:

Our favorite things and places to eat:

Other Notes:

_____
_____
_____
_____
_____
_____
_____
_____
_____

A drawing or photo of the favorite part of our stay:

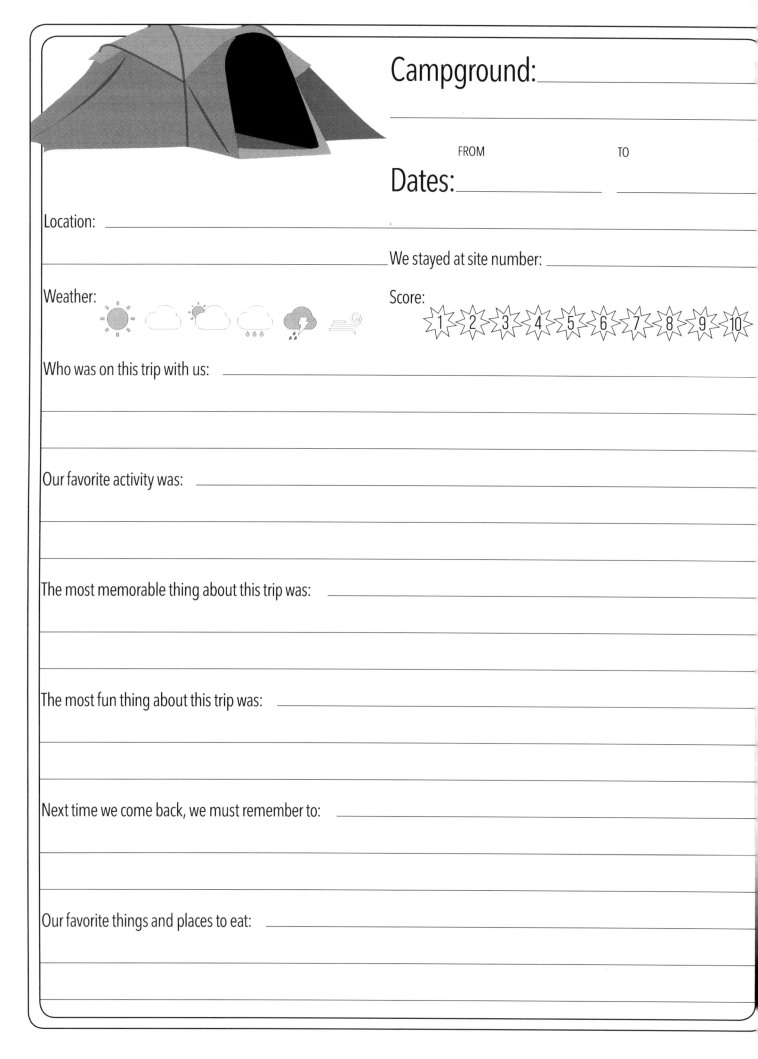

Campground: _____

_____

FROM   TO

Dates: _____   _____

Location: _____

_____ We stayed at site number: _____

Weather: Score:

1 2 3 4 5 6 7 8 9 10

Who was on this trip with us: _____

_____

_____

Our favorite activity was: _____

_____

_____

The most memorable thing about this trip was: _____

_____

_____

The most fun thing about this trip was: _____

_____

_____

Next time we come back, we must remember to: _____

_____

_____

Our favorite things and places to eat: _____

_____

_____

Other Notes:

_____
_____
_____
_____
_____
_____
_____
_____
_____
_____

A drawing or photo of the favorite part of our stay:

Campground: _____

_____

FROM _____ TO _____

Dates: _____ _____

Location: _____

_____

We stayed at site number: _____

Weather: ☀ ☁ ⛅ 🌧 ⛈ 🌬

Score: 1 2 3 4 5 6 7 8 9 10

Who was on this trip with us: _____

_____

_____

Our favorite activity was: _____

_____

_____

The most memorable thing about this trip was: _____

_____

_____

The most fun thing about this trip was: _____

_____

_____

Next time we come back, we must remember to: _____

_____

_____

Our favorite things and places to eat: _____

_____

_____

Other Notes:

_____

_____

_____

_____

_____

_____

_____

_____

_____

A drawing or photo of the favorite part of our stay:

Campground: _____

FROM   TO

Dates: _____   _____

Location: _____

_____ We stayed at site number: _____

Weather: Score:

1 2 3 4 5 6 7 8 9 10

Who was on this trip with us: _____

_____

_____

Our favorite activity was: _____

_____

_____

The most memorable thing about this trip was: _____

_____

_____

The most fun thing about this trip was: _____

_____

_____

Next time we come back, we must remember to: _____

_____

_____

Our favorite things and places to eat: _____

_____

_____

Other Notes:

_____
_____
_____
_____
_____
_____
_____
_____
_____
_____

A drawing or photo of the favorite part of our stay:

Campground:

FROM   TO

Dates:

Location: _____

We stayed at site number: _____

Weather: ☀ ☁ ⛅ 🌧 ⛈ 🌬

Score: 1 2 3 4 5 6 7 8 9 10

Who was on this trip with us: _____

Our favorite activity was: _____

The most memorable thing about this trip was: _____

The most fun thing about this trip was: _____

Next time we come back, we must remember to: _____

Our favorite things and places to eat: _____

Other Notes:

A drawing or photo of the favorite part of our stay:

Campground:_____

_____

FROM   TO

Dates:_____   _____

Location: _____

_____

We stayed at site number: _____

Weather:

Score:

1 2 3 4 5 6 7 8 9 10

Who was on this trip with us: _____

_____

_____

Our favorite activity was: _____

_____

_____

The most memorable thing about this trip was: _____

_____

_____

The most fun thing about this trip was: _____

_____

_____

Next time we come back, we must remember to: _____

_____

_____

Our favorite things and places to eat: _____

_____

_____

Other Notes:

_____
_____
_____
_____
_____
_____
_____
_____
_____

A drawing or photo of the favorite part of our stay:

Campground:

FROM   TO

Dates:

Location:

We stayed at site number:

Weather:

Score: 1 2 3 4 5 6 7 8 9 10

Who was on this trip with us:

Our favorite activity was:

The most memorable thing about this trip was:

The most fun thing about this trip was:

Next time we come back, we must remember to:

Our favorite things and places to eat:

Other Notes:

A drawing or photo of the favorite part of our stay:

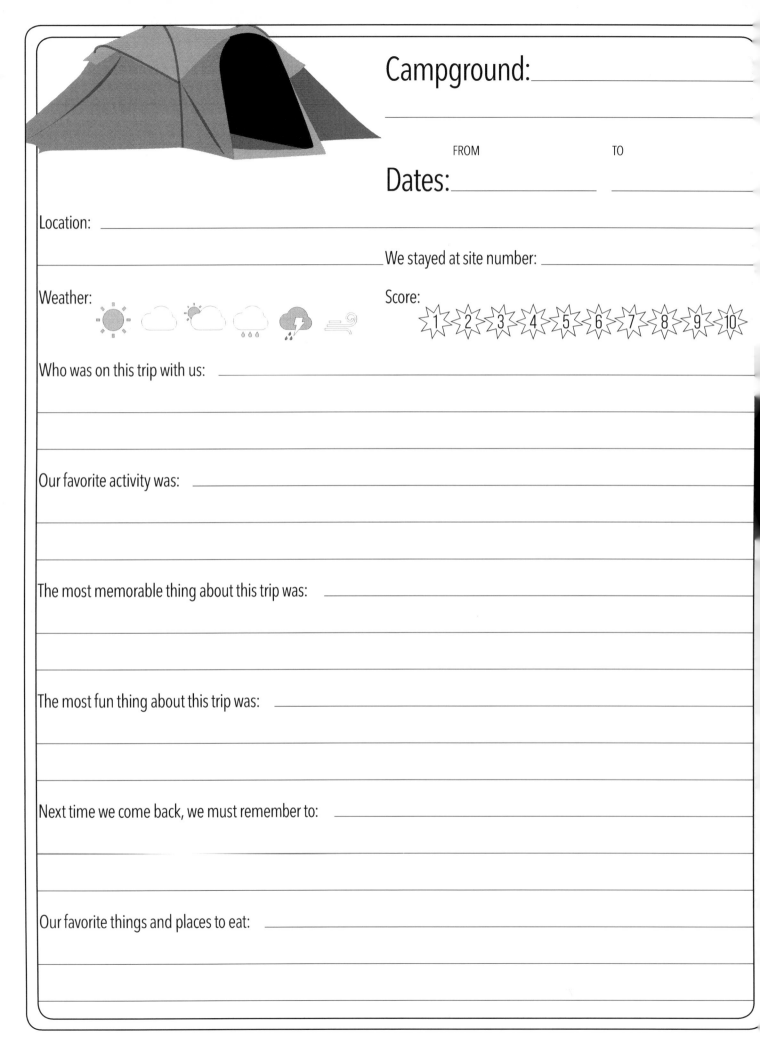

Campground: _____

_____

FROM   TO

Dates: _____   _____

Location: _____

_____

We stayed at site number: _____

Weather: ☀ ☁ 🌤 🌧 ⛈ 🌬

Score: 1 2 3 4 5 6 7 8 9 10

Who was on this trip with us: _____

_____

_____

Our favorite activity was: _____

_____

_____

The most memorable thing about this trip was: _____

_____

_____

The most fun thing about this trip was: _____

_____

_____

Next time we come back, we must remember to: _____

_____

_____

Our favorite things and places to eat: _____

_____

Other Notes:

A drawing or photo of the favorite part of our stay:

Campground:_____

_____

FROM   TO

Dates:_____ _____

Location: _____

_____ We stayed at site number: _____

Weather: ☀ ☁ ⛅ 🌧 ⛈ 🌬   Score: 1 2 3 4 5 6 7 8 9 10

Who was on this trip with us: _____

_____

_____

Our favorite activity was: _____

_____

_____

The most memorable thing about this trip was: _____

_____

_____

The most fun thing about this trip was: _____

_____

_____

Next time we come back, we must remember to: _____

_____

_____

Our favorite things and places to eat: _____

_____

_____

Other Notes:

A drawing or photo of the favorite part of our stay:

Campground: _____

_____

FROM _____ TO _____

Dates: _____

Location: _____

_____

We stayed at site number: _____

Weather: ☀ ☁ ⛅ 🌧 ⛈ 🌬

Score: 1 2 3 4 5 6 7 8 9 10

Who was on this trip with us: _____

_____

_____

Our favorite activity was: _____

_____

_____

The most memorable thing about this trip was: _____

_____

_____

The most fun thing about this trip was: _____

_____

_____

Next time we come back, we must remember to: _____

_____

_____

Our favorite things and places to eat: _____

_____

_____

Other Notes:

A drawing or photo of the favorite part of our stay:

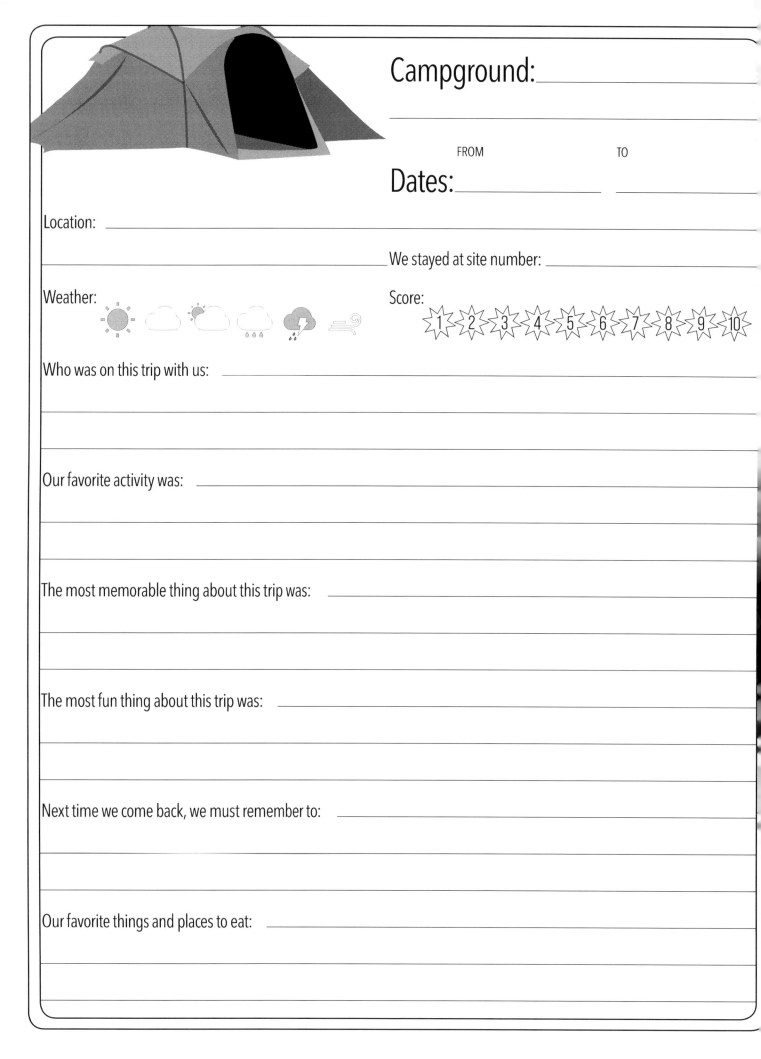

Campground:_____

Dates: FROM_____ TO_____

Location: _____

We stayed at site number: _____

Weather:

Score: 1 2 3 4 5 6 7 8 9 10

Who was on this trip with us: _____

Our favorite activity was: _____

The most memorable thing about this trip was: _____

The most fun thing about this trip was: _____

Next time we come back, we must remember to: _____

Our favorite things and places to eat: _____

Other Notes:

A drawing or photo of the favorite part of our stay:

Campground: _____

_____

FROM _____ TO _____

Dates: _____ _____

Location: _____

_____ We stayed at site number: _____

Weather: ☀ ☁ ⛅ 🌧 ⛈ 💨   Score: 1 2 3 4 5 6 7 8 9 10

Who was on this trip with us: _____

_____

_____

Our favorite activity was: _____

_____

_____

The most memorable thing about this trip was: _____

_____

_____

The most fun thing about this trip was: _____

_____

_____

Next time we come back, we must remember to: _____

_____

_____

Our favorite things and places to eat: _____

_____

_____

Other Notes:

A drawing or photo of the favorite part of our stay:

Campground: _____

_____

FROM   TO

Dates: _____   _____

Location: _____

_____ We stayed at site number: _____

Weather: Score:

1 2 3 4 5 6 7 8 9 10

Who was on this trip with us: _____

_____

_____

Our favorite activity was: _____

_____

_____

The most memorable thing about this trip was: _____

_____

_____

The most fun thing about this trip was: _____

_____

_____

Next time we come back, we must remember to: _____

_____

_____

Our favorite things and places to eat: _____

_____

_____

Other Notes:

_____
_____
_____
_____
_____
_____
_____
_____
_____
_____

A drawing or photo of the favorite part of our stay:

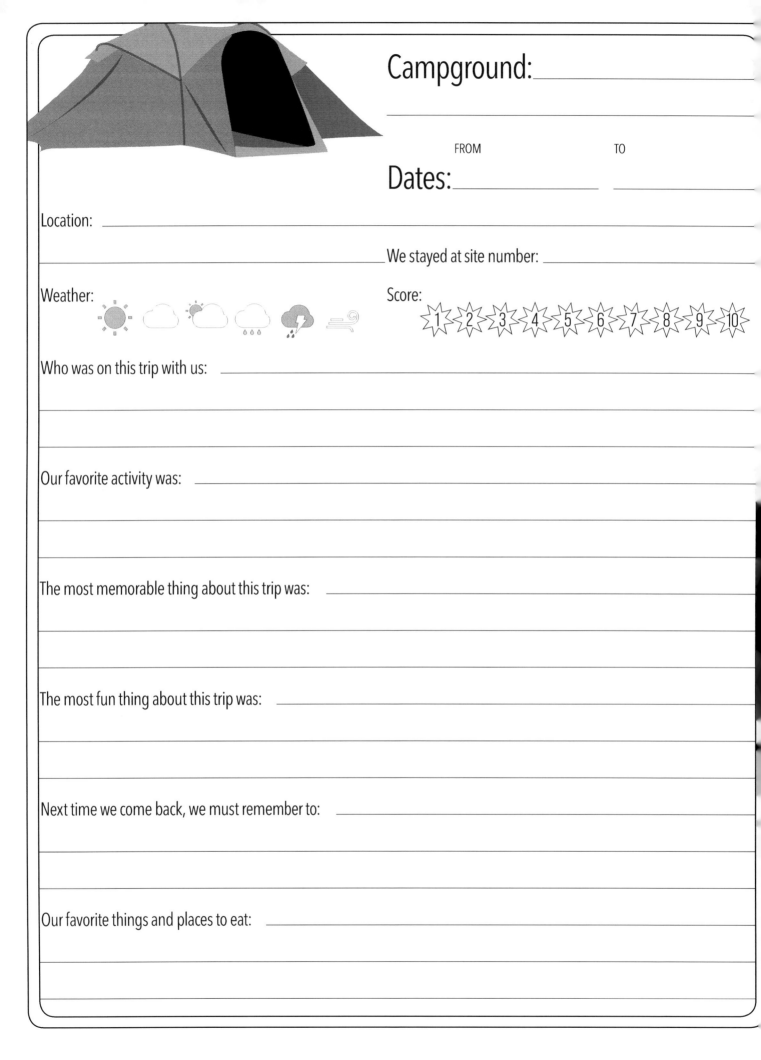

Campground:

FROM　　　　　　　　　TO
Dates:

Location: _____

_____ We stayed at site number: _____

Weather: ☀ ☁ ⛅ 🌧 ⛈ 🌬

Score: 1 2 3 4 5 6 7 8 9 10

Who was on this trip with us: _____

_____

_____

Our favorite activity was: _____

_____

_____

The most memorable thing about this trip was: _____

_____

_____

The most fun thing about this trip was: _____

_____

_____

Next time we come back, we must remember to: _____

_____

_____

Our favorite things and places to eat: _____

_____

_____

Other Notes:

A drawing or photo of the favorite part of our stay:

Campground:

FROM   TO

Dates:

Location:

We stayed at site number:

Weather:

Score: 1 2 3 4 5 6 7 8 9 10

Who was on this trip with us:

Our favorite activity was:

The most memorable thing about this trip was:

The most fun thing about this trip was:

Next time we come back, we must remember to:

Our favorite things and places to eat:

Other Notes:

A drawing or photo of the favorite part of our stay:

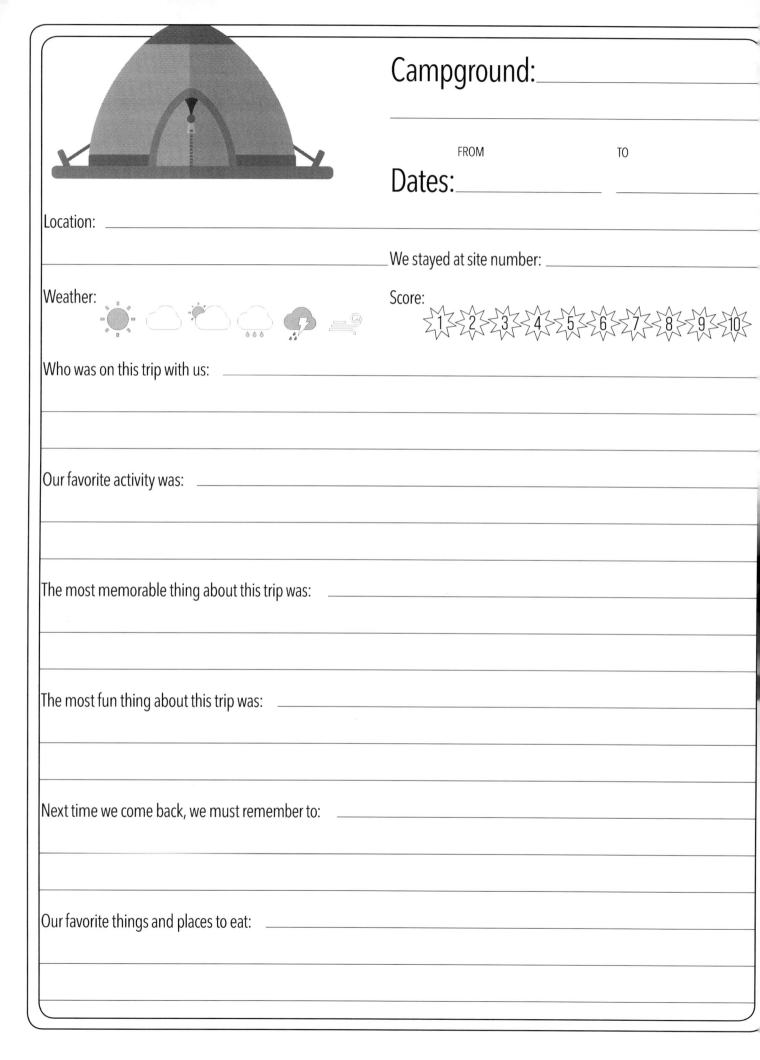

Campground:

FROM   TO

Dates:

Location:

We stayed at site number:

Weather:

Score:

1 2 3 4 5 6 7 8 9 10

Who was on this trip with us:

Our favorite activity was:

The most memorable thing about this trip was:

The most fun thing about this trip was:

Next time we come back, we must remember to:

Our favorite things and places to eat:

Other Notes:

A drawing or photo of the favorite part of our stay:

Made in the USA
Middletown, DE
28 August 2021